Minnie
&
The Better Den

Carmel Noel

illustrated by tt

Minnie & The Better Den

Copyright © 2020 Carmel Noel.

For information contact:

Carmel Noel at carmelgnoel@gmail.com

Written by Carmel Noel

Illustrated by Theresa Tribus

Edited by Daniel Brown

ISBN 9780578614212 (Hardcover Edition)
9781087860985 (Softcover Edition)

Library of Congress Control Number: 2020901003

10 9 8 7 6 5 4 3 2 1

First Edition: January 2020

If you recognize yourself in this story, this book is for you. Psalm 34:18

— cn

for pinecone

— tt

Minnie was only a wee pup when she learned that some human-folk don't know how to play...

She was only a few weeks old when she left the noisy place
with the bright lights and metal cages, and met the small
human-folk boy she would know as Rain, and his big
human-folk keeper, Thump.

Rain held her close to his chest the whole time they were in the Rattling Machine. Thump barked at Rain in a way that scared Minnie, even though she didn't quite understand what he was saying.

Minnie tried to play with Thump's big round toy, but he bore his large yellow teeth at her and she decided it was best to let him play alone.

When they arrived at their human-folk den, Minnie got to sniff lots of new things. She sniffed the doormat, and the sofa, and the big barrel that Thump liked to make go "BOOM".

She got a strong whiff of no-good, and tried to taste a small corner of the angry, snapping snack, which she quickly learned was very dangerous for small paws like hers.

Thump made Rain cry with his big paws time and time again, and Minnie began to wonder if the snapping snack wasn't the only dangerous thing in her new den.

During the days, Thump played rough and liked to push Minnie off the comfy arm of the sofa. But the days always passed into evenings and when the sun went down, Minnie spent the nights burrowed deep in Rain's arms. His tiny teardrops soaked her fur, leaving it salty and stiff.

In the dark, Rain told Minnie stories about Jesus. She often wondered what sort of creature this Jesus could be. Thump liked to bark something that sounded like his name when he was angry and waving his big paws, but Rain would whisper it tenderly in the dead of night. Minnie chose to believe that Rain knew better than Thump, because the Jesus in his stories was full of love, not anger.

One day, while Thump and Rain were out of the den, Minnie decided to try and find Jesus. She carried the big BOOM-barrel in her mouth, just in case, even though she did not know how to use it, and set off on her journey

Minnie made it as far as the cage door near the road when she felt something bad on her back. She cried and tried to swing the big BOOM-barrel, but she was too slow and Thump just snatched it from between her teeth. Thump was very angry! He didn't seem to want Minnie to find Jesus, or to use his big BOOM-barrel.

Minnie doesn't like to remember much of what happened after she left the den.

Her belly and teeth ached as she ran away from Rattling Machines on the road, and wandered through the thick woods.

Minnie often thought about Rain and wondered if Jesus
would be able to take her back to him.
But when Minnie found Jesus, she learned that he had
other plans.

He was like the human-folk, except he never barked or grabbed. She saw him sitting under a tree and was surprised to hear him say her name before she even told him what it was.

Jesus scooped Minnie's aching body into his arms, and his tears fell like a mist, and soothed her. He told her that he had a better den for her to live in, and that Rain would know when to join her when he was older.

Jesus carried Minnie for what felt like a very long time. He picked berries along the way and fed them to her. Minnie drank the nectar from the sweet honeysuckle Jesus gave to her and, even though it often rained, she felt warm in his arms.

At night Jesus made them beds of wildflowers, and laid a gentle hand on her as they slept under bright stars. Jesus snored sometimes, but Minnie didn't mind.

Eventually, they reached a wide-open space, surrounded by hills rolling into hills. There, right in the middle, was the biggest and most beautiful den Minnie had ever seen. It was covered in big pictures that sparkled in the sunlight, and Minnie could hear peaceful music coming from inside.

Gently, Jesus crouched down with Minnie in front of
the den and told her she was safe. Even though she had
seen, felt and sniffed bad things, Jesus explained that
there were only good things in her new den. Minnie
trusted Jesus and knew he was telling her the truth.

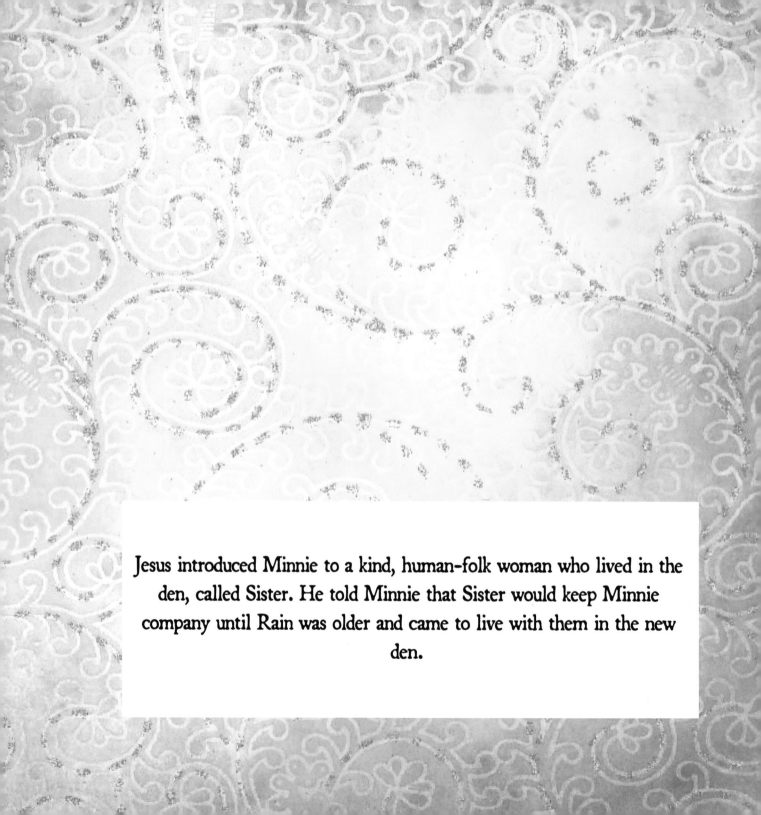

Jesus introduced Minnie to a kind, human-folk woman who lived in the den, called Sister. He told Minnie that Sister would keep Minnie company until Rain was older and came to live with them in the new den.

As he embraced her, Jesus told Minnie that, even though she may not always be able to see him, he would always be nearby, and he would always love her.

Dear Little One,

I hope you have enjoyed reading Minnie & The Better Den! Being the wonderfully curious creation that you are, I am sure you have a few questions. I did my best to answer a few that you may have here, and to provide you with where you can find examples in the Bible! There are more answers in the Bible than I could possibly provide in this book. You can ask a grown-up who loves you to help you find them! Remember that just like Jesus told Minnie that, even though she may not always be able to see him, he would always be nearby, and he would always love her, the same is true for you. You are loved and Jesus is never far away!

Why do some grown-ups say the name of Jesus when they are angry?

When grown-ups say that name in anger, that is what the bible calls using the Lord's name in vain- that is a sin, like lying or stealing! I am sorry to tell you that you will probably hear a lot of grown-ups do this. Did you know that it says in the Bible that His name is ranked above every other name in the whole world and that his name has real power in it to do good?

Did Jesus really snore?!

e cannot be completely sure if Jesus snored or not, but
 could have! He got tired and slept because He was as
man as you are!
hn 4:6 1 Timothy 2:5

Can Jesus really cry?

Yes! Jesus can cry, just like you. The Bible says so!
John 11:35

Can His name be used against me?

No way! In fact, you can use it to protect yourself from scary things! When you speak
to God it is called praying; just like you can say the name of your parent or friend and
they will listen to you, you can say the name of Jesus and He will listen to everything
you want to tell him and protect you from your fears.
Luke 10:17 John 16:23–24, Proverbs 18:10

How did he know her name?

sus was not only a man; He is our Lord God! He knew her name before
 was even born, and he knows yours too!
aiah 43:1

Would Jesus really carry Minnie like that?

In the Bible, there are many places that say God will carry those He cares
for.
Psalm 91:11-12, Luke 4:11 Matthew 4:6 Isaiah 63:9 Isaiah 40:11 Deuteronomy
1:31